FAM[illegible]
ALBUM

by Alan Ayckbourn

SAMUEL FRENCH

ISBN 978-0-573-00025-6

concordtheatricals.co.uk
concordtheatricals.com

FOR AMATEUR PRODUCTION ENQUIRIES

United Kingdom and World
excluding North America
licensing@concordtheatricals.co.uk
020-7054-7298

Each title is subject to availability from Concord Theatricals, depending upon country of performance.

This work is published by Samuel French, an imprint of Concord Theatricals Ltd.

Professional Performing Rights: applications for performance by professionals in any medium and in any language throughout the world should be addressed to Casarotto Ramsay & Associates Ltd, www.casarotto.co.uk email: rights@casarotto.co.uk.

FAMILY ALBUM was first produced by the Stephen Joseph Theatre, Scarborough (Round auditorium), on 6th September, 2022. The performance was directed by Alan Ayckbourn, with set and costume design by Kevin Jenkins and lighting by Jason Taylor. Sound by Alan Ayckbourn and Sound Associate Paul Stear. The Deputy Stage Manager was Sue Volans. The two Assistant Stage Managers, Jude Deeno and David Lomond, also played the non-speaking removal men roles. The cast was as follows:

JOHN STANTON .... Antony Eden
PEGGY STANTON .... Georgia Burnell
SANDRA DICKENS .... Frances Marshall
ALISON STANTON-HICKS .... Elizabeth Boag
JESS STANTON-HICKS .... Tanya-Loretta Dee
TWO REMOVAL MEN .... Jude Deeno & David Lomond

CHARACTERS

<u>**February, 1952. Moving In**</u>

JOHN STANTON – 29, a warehouse supervisor, ex RAF

PEGGY STANTON – 27, a housewife, his wife

<u>**July, 1992. The Birthday Party**</u>

SANDRA DICKENS – 48, a former primary teacher, daughter of John and Peggy

<u>**November 2022. Moving Out**</u>

ALISON STANTON-HICKS – 40, a freelance graphic designer, daughter of Sandra

JESS STANTON-HICKS – 38, her partner, a BBC researcher

<u>**c1952 and 2022**</u>

TWO REMOVAL MEN – non-speaking and very different in both time periods

SETTING

The front living room of 27, Byfield Crescent, SW19.

TIME

Between the years 1952 and 2022.

The three time periods are often seen simultaneously.

In **ACT TWO**, in all cases, a certain time has elapsed.

AUTHOR'S NOTES

The following serves as a family tree, showing all the unseen, offstage family members as well as the ones we will see on stage, and referencing their point in time during each phase of the action.

February, 1952. Moving In

The Grandparents:
JOHN STANTON – 29, a warehouse supervisor, ex RAF,
PEGGY (MARGARET) STANTON (NEÉ CADDICK) – 27, a housewife, his wife

Their Children:
SANDRA (SANDY) – 8
RICHARD (DICKIE) – 6

July, 1992. The Birthday Party

The Parents:
SANDRA (SANDY) DICKENS (NEÉ STANTON) – 48, a former primary teacher
JEREMY DICKENS – 45, her husband, a sports master

Their Children:
TERENCE – 14
EDWARD – 12
ALISON – 10
Sandra's parents, **JOHN** – 69 and **PEGGY** – 67 are in a retirement home

Sandra's brother, **RICHARD** – 46, is now a dispensing chemist

November 2022. Moving Out

The Children:
ALISON STANTON-HICKS – 40, a freelance graphic designer
JESS STANTON-HICKS – 38, her partner, a BBC researcher
Alison's brother, **TERENCE** – 44, is now a QC
Alison's brother, **EDWARD** – 18, deceased
Alison's parents are both deceased. **JEREMY** – 70 and **SANDRA** – 78
Alison's grandparents are both deceased. **JOHN** – 90 and **MARGARET** – 96

TWO REMOVAL MEN – c 1952 and 2022 (non-speaking and very different in both time periods)

ACT ONE

(The front living room of 27, Byfield Crescent, SW19.)

(The action moves freely from time period to time period.)

(There is a single doorway, common to all periods, leading to the rest of the house, upstairs and downstairs as well as to the front door. A front window looking out onto the street.)

(The room is devoid of furniture at the start in the earliest period, 1952. The **STANTONS**, **JOHN** *and* **PEGGY**, *are in the process of moving in on a late February afternoon.* **PEGGY**, *a twenty-seven year old mother and housewife, enters from the hall. She is unfamiliar with her new house and moves rather cautiously to the centre of the empty room. It is clearly unheated and she has opted to keep her coat on. She stands for a moment looking round her with a certain pleasure and excitement.)*

PEGGY. *(To herself.)* Hello, room. Hello, house.

(From the hall, the 1952 doorbell rings.)

(Starting, clearly unfamiliar with this.) Oh! Doorbell!

(She hurries to the window and takes a quick peek out.)

They're here already!

(She goes out to the front door.)

(As soon as she has gone, the lights change and it is now a July afternoon with the sun streaming through the front window. In the hall, a phone is ringing insistently.)

(We are now in the 'middle' period, July 1992, where there is currently a child's tenth birthday party in progress in the adjoining dining room. This room is accessed by way of a double doorway recently knocked through by the owners during the previous decade. It is therefore non-existent to the residents occupying the house during the earlier period in February 1952.)

(As the phone rings on insistently, the doors to the dining room open and **SANDRA**, *a mother of three in her late forties, sticks her head out to listen. She is clutching a glass of what could be orange squash but is probably something far stronger. During the course of the afternoon she becomes steadily more intoxicated. She was, twenty years ago, what was known in those days euphemistically as 'a child of the sixties'. Behind her can be heard the chatter of a dozen or so excited children's voices.)*

SANDRA. *(Calling back to them.)* Sshh! Sshh! Sshh! Just a minute, kids! Sshh, a moment!

(The dining room sounds die down slightly.)

(Confirming the phone ring.) Yes! You're quite right, it is, it's ringing! You're quite right!... What's that? ... Yes, it could, it could well be Daddy now, Alison,

couldn't it? Naughty Daddy's late again isn't he? After he promised this morning. Wait there quietly, everyone please! Jennifer, you're in charge remember! Jennifer's in charge, everyone so do exactly as Jennifer tells you! Ali darling, it's your party, help Jennifer to look after your guests, please! See they behave properly! Mummy won't be a moment!

(She closes the dining room doors and the sounds cut off from within.)

(To herself, catching her breath.) Jesus wept! How much longer?

(As the phone continues to ring, she makes her way to the hall in a somewhat uncoordinated fashion and goes out. After a moment, it stops ringing.)

(The lights change back again to February 1952 and **PEGGY** *re-enters having let in the* **REMOVAL MEN**. *During the next, she busily divides her attention between the window, checking on the unloading progress outside and the hallway, as the* **REMOVAL MEN** *pass with various neatly labelled cartons and tea chests.)*

PEGGY. *(Calling behind her to the* **REMOVAL MEN**.*)* That one has a red label and it goes in the kitchen, as well. Anything with a red label goes in the kitchen. Straight down the hall again, please...

(A **REMOVAL MAN** *appears in the hall doorway presenting her with a blue labelled tea chest.)*

(Distracted.) Yes, same again, kitchen please. *(Calling him back.)* No, wait! Wait! Just a tick! Hasn't that got a blue label? That's meant for the dining room! Next door in the dining room! Next door on the right! *(Calling*

after him.) If we ever find where on earth I packed the kettle, I'll make you that cup of tea I promised! *(To herself.)* If we've got any tea to spare, that is. I've a nasty feeling we're running out.

(Another box is presented.)

(Checking this.) What's this, then? Ah, yes. Yellow label? Most important! Children's room! Precious toys! Mustn't lose the toys whatever we do! Upstairs! Children's room! Top of the stairs, turn left, small back bedroom.

(The **REMOVAL MAN** *departs.)*

(Calling after him.) Where your colleagues have just taken the bunk beds.

*(***SANDRA** *returns from the hall, now holding the cordless phone. As she crosses back to the dining room doors, the lights change briefly.)*

SANDRA. *(Muttering to herself as she crosses.)* Bloody wrong numbers! Where the hell have you got to, Jerry, you bugger? Coping here all on my own! You promised me, you promised...

(She opens the dining room doors.)

(A burst of children's voices from within.)

(As she does so.) Sorry, kids! False alarm! Alison's daddy's done a runner! *(To herself.)* Yet again!

(She closes the door behind her and the sounds cut off.)

*(***PEGGY** *remains anxiously at the window. Needless to say, neither woman is aware of the other, nor indeed are any of the characters from the different time periods. As the lights change back to 1952, a* **REMOVAL MAN** *backs*

on supporting one end of a fairly large three-seater sofa, bearing a green label.)

PEGGY. *(Prattling excitedly.)* Ah, now! Yes, right. Green label! That does go in here! Do mind the new paintwork, won't you? If there's even so much as the teeniest scratch, my husband will go absolutely mad. Everything's just so sparkling new, it's terrifying. I mean once the children run loose in the place, it's never going to last, is it? *(She laughs.)*

(During the last, the **REMOVAL MEN** *have struggled to move the sofa to the middle of the room. It's clearly quite heavy. They wait.)*

(Chattering on excitedly.) It's just that this is our first place together, you see, our first proper home of our very own, you see, so it's all rather special, just at present. Up till now, as you probably noticed, we've been camping out with my parents, just the two rooms. We have been ever since the war. But now, thank heavens, we're able to get back to some sort of normality, at last. Get on with our own lives.

(The **REMOVAL MEN** *continue to wait.)*

(Considering the best position.) Yes. I think the best place for that is against that wall there, don't you?

(They move the sofa to the wall.)

(As they do so.) I mean, don't get me wrong, my parents have been wonderful, tremendously supportive. And so generous. Most of this furniture used to be theirs and they've simply gifted it to us. Like that sofa for instance – *(Re-considering.)* – No, I'm sorry, I think on second thoughts, it's better against that wall there, would you mind? I'm awfully sorry –

(They move the sofa to the other wall.)

(As they do so.) I mean, since my husband left the Air Force he's landed a pretty good job, of course, we mustn't complain, we've been awfully lucky but by the time he'd dealt with the mortgage and so on, we could never have afforded a sofa like that, not in a month of Sundays. *(Reconsidering again.)*. No, that's not right either. It doesn't belong there, not at all. We were right the first time. Sorry, would you mind, as you were before –?

> *(The* **REMOVAL MEN** *move the sofa back again.)*

(As they do so.) No, I mean, that sofa is genuine Victorian. It was built to last. Not like some of the cheap utility stuff these days. The Victorians knew how to make them, didn't they? Good old British craftsmanship, solid mahogany, best quality horsehair – no that's still not right, I'm sorry, I think what we'll need to do is wait till we get everything else in here before we finally decide. I'll need to consult my husband, he should be home from work any minute now. Thank you so much, do carry on with your unloading, won't you?

> *(The* **REMOVAL MEN** *move back towards the door.)*

(A sudden second thought.) Oh, I say, I say! Before you go, I know you're going to hate me for this, you're really going to loathe me, but would you be terribly sweet and just try it in the middle here? Thank you so much.

> *(The* **REMOVAL MEN** *return and start to move the sofa once again.)*

(As they do so, laughing.) Sorry. I know you must be thinking this is the very last time we move house for this woman! The very last time! I think it's so important, isn't it, to get these things right? I mean, in the end, you have to live with it, don't you?

(The **REMOVAL MEN** *place the sofa in the middle of the room, facing the window.)*

(Making final adjustments.) Little bit towards me.

(They make the adjustment.)

Little bit more. Whoaa! Little bit back. That's it! Whoaa! That's perfect. Absolutely spot-on. Thank you. I can't thank you enough. Thank you so much.

(The **REMOVAL MEN** *leave.* **PEGGY** *studies the sofa for a second and then sits on it.)*

No, this is perfect. We can sit here and look out on the street, can't we? *(Craning her neck.)* Just about. No, this is lovely. Lovely.

(The lights change back to the 1992 state as the phone starts ringing again in the hall. This time it quickly cuts off and, in a moment, **SANDRA** *comes out of the dining room, accompanied by the usual children's hubbub, this time with the phone clamped to one ear, covering the other with her free hand.* **PEGGY** *sits, oblivious, on the sofa in her own dream world.)*

SANDRA. ...well, where are you exactly? Jerry, it's her bloody birthday... you knew it was her birthday... yes you bloody did because I reminded you this morning... don't forget Alison's party... that was the last thing I said to you as you walked out the door... now she keeps asking, "Where's Daddy? Is Daddy coming?"... Well, when are you coming home? When can I tell her to expect you? ...Jesus, Jerry, of course she does. She worships the bloody ground you walk on, you know that... she doesn't want me, she wants you... only you're never here for her, are you...? No, never. You weren't even there for her christening, were you?

*(**SANDRA** goes out into the hall, as she talks. The lights change back to 1952.)*

PEGGY. *(Murmuring happily to herself.)* Oh, this is heaven! It's such a peaceful house... so peaceful. We're going to be so happy here, I know we are.

*(The **REMOVAL MEN** return carrying a writing desk and stool. They pause in the doorway.)*

Ah! Yes, please, that's another green label, well done, that's in here, thank you. *(Considering.)* I think – just along that wall there, don't you?

*(The **REMOVAL MEN** place the writing desk in position.)*

(As they do so.) I was just thinking, this sofa's in the perfect position, you know. Perfect. It means that from here I can see out of the – Oh, look! There he is now, my husband's just arrived. *(Waving and mouthing.)* Hello, darling!

*(The **REMOVAL MEN** move back to the door, nearly colliding with **JOHN**, a brisk, energetic man, a couple of years older than his wife and clearly ex-services. He is holding the day's edition of* The Evening News.*)*

JOHN. *(As he enters.)* Excuse me, have you seen my – Ah! Here you are, darling, you're in here!

PEGGY. *(Happily greeting him.)* Darling!

JOHN. *(Jocularly.)* What are you up to then, old thing? Lounging about as usual, I see.

PEGGY. Just trying out our sofa. I think I've found the perfect place for it, don't you?

JOHN. How are these chaps getting on, then? Everything unloaded, is it?

PEGGY. I think very nearly. It's all been very efficient. Largely thanks to your brilliant idea with all the coloured labels. It's been quite hectic, here. I'd no idea we had so much stuff.

JOHN. Well, your parent's furniture took up most of the van...

PEGGY. We needed furniture, darling...

JOHN. Yes we certainly did, but...

PEGGY. ...we couldn't have survived without furniture, could we...?

JOHN. ...No, not at all, but...

PEGGY. ...We couldn't all sit on cardboard boxes, could we?

JOHN. Yes, yes, point taken, darling. Anyway, sorry to leave you to cope on your own, old thing. Needs must. We've been having a massive stock-take. Took a bit of getting used to for everyone, since I introduced the new filing system.

PEGGY. Well, you have to go to work, of course you do. We're all relying on you, darling.

JOHN. *(Sitting beside her.)* No, don't get me wrong, it was most generous of your parents, much appreciated. Especially the bed.

PEGGY. *(Giggling slightly.)* Yes, 'specially the bed. *(She nuzzles him affectionately.)* And, come to think of it, I'm glad we still have this sofa, aren't you?

JOHN. How do you mean?

PEGGY. You remember? Whenever you came home on leave, when it was in Mummy and Daddy's drawing room, we used to...

JOHN. *(Smiling.)* Oh, yes, yes, of course. Yes. So we did.

PEGGY. *(Patting the sofa.)* I think this sofa was partly responsible for Sandra, if you recall...

JOHN. Scene of the crime, eh?

PEGGY. *(Frowning.)* No! Hardly a crime, darling. I wouldn't call it a crime... we were just too nervous to go up to my bedroom, weren't we?

JOHN. Well, you were...

PEGGY. I was...

JOHN. I blame you entirely for that.

PEGGY. *(Indignantly.)* Me? Why me?

JOHN. If you hadn't insisted on making such an infernal din about it...

PEGGY. *(Somewhat embarrassed.)* I couldn't help that, it was – natural, wasn't it?

JOHN. Natural?

PEGGY. I mean, for a woman. It's in a woman's nature for most of them.

JOHN. *(Amused.)* Well, I won't argue with you there. From my experience, it's in a woman's nature to make a din about most things... *(He laughs.)*

PEGGY. *(Laughing affectionately.)* Oh, you're terrible, you're such a tease!

JOHN. No, they were particularly thin walls in your parent's house... I still remember your father snoring through the wall next to me, when I was home on leave... it was almost like having him in the same bed as us.

PEGGY. Poor Daddy!

(The **REMOVAL MEN** *start to back in with a heavy sideboard.)*

JOHN. *(Seeing them.)* Yes, come on in, chaps! Green label! That belongs in here, thank you.

PEGGY. Oh, not the dining room?

JOHN. No, not blue label. In here. It's green label. Definitely in here.

PEGGY. I thought that might be better in the dining room? I thought perhaps it should be blue label…

JOHN. No, darling, green label, green label! *(To the* **REMOVAL MEN.***)* Carry on, chaps! Ignore this woman! Just along that wall there, please.

PEGGY. Are you sure, darling?

JOHN. Not according to the plan, darling. We did draw up a colour-coded master plan, if you remember.

PEGGY. Well, you drew up a master plan.

JOHN. *(To the* **REMOVAL MEN.***)* Thank you, that's perfect. *(To her.)* Don't you agree, darling, it looks splendid there?

(The **REMOVAL MEN** *depart again.)*

PEGGY. Yes, fine. It's just I always associated it with the dining room. It sat there in Mummy and Daddy's dining room, for years, ever since I was little. We used to keep all the cutlery and the condiments in there. Along with the best crockery. It was just so handy at mealtimes. My sister and I used to love laying the table, whenever Mummy allowed us to.

JOHN. Yes, I do remember it in their dining room. In my opinion, it never really looked quite right in there. Don't complain now, it's where we put it on the plan. Where we agreed. It's perfect where it is. Where have you put the plan, by the way?

PEGGY. *(Guiltily.)* I've – I think I may have mislaid it…

JOHN. Mislaid it?

PEGGY. I'm sorry, darling, I put it down somewhere, I can't think where I –

JOHN. For heaven's sake, Pegs! You dozy bumpkin! I spent half the night drawing that up!

PEGGY. *(Unhappily.)* Yes, I know you did. I can't think where I left it.

JOHN. Everything was marked out to the nearest inch...

PEGGY. I think I may have left it back at the other house.

JOHN. ...all drawn up to scale. One in twenty.

PEGGY. It did all seem rather – if you don't mind my saying so – rather clinical, somehow. If you know what I mean. It was like a sort of military operation, really...

JOHN. That's precisely what this is, Pegs, a military operation. It requires precision planning. Everything in its proper place. Everything belongs where it belongs.

PEGGY. I just thought it would be nice if we simply moved everything in and then just sort of decided. Once we were in here. Improvised, you know. As the mood took us.

JOHN. *(Blankly.)* Improvised?

PEGGY. Let it all – you know – choose for itself. Willy-nilly.

JOHN. Willy-nilly?

PEGGY. Let things go where they feel they're – most happy.

JOHN. Right-o. We'd better go round and ask them then, haven't we?

PEGGY. No, don't be silly...

JOHN. I warn you, if we start asking each stick of furniture where it would prefer to go, we're going to end up living in a very peculiar house, if that's your plan of action, darling. Kitchen stove over here, kids' bunk beds over there, your dressing table in the middle of the hall there...

PEGGY. ...no, no, no, that's silly...

JOHN. ...it'll be absolute chaos, if every item of furniture was allowed to go where it feels like, we'd probably finish up sleeping on the front lawn.

PEGGY. No, John, you know what I'm saying, don't be so mean...

JOHN. Yes, I know perfectly well what you're saying, you daft little darling, but then you know perfectly well what I'm saying, too, don't you? So don't start pretending to be dopier than you are. *(Seriously.)* This is our first proper home together, Pegs, as a family. The four of us. You, me, Dickie and Sandy. Now we're no longer glorified lodgers, tiptoeing about the place, for ever talking in hushed whispers. Think of it, Pegs, we're under our own roof at last! No more thin partition walls, no more shushing the kids because granddad's having his nap. We're free, aren't we? Free to do as we choose?

PEGGY. *(Catching his tone.)* Yes, quite right, we're free!

*(**JOHN** rises. He studies the room. He stares at the writing desk and shakes his head.)*

What's the matter?

JOHN. *(Staring at the writing desk.)* No, that's not right! Quite wrong!

PEGGY. What's that?

(He crosses to the door.)

JOHN. *(Calling.)* I say! I say! Have you a moment, one of you?

*(The **REMOVAL MEN** return.)*

That desk is in the wrong place. It should go across the window there. Would you mind?

PEGGY. *(Dismayed at the suggestion.)* Oh! Are you sure?

(The **REMOVAL MEN** *move it into position, more or less directly between them and the window.)*

JOHN. That's it! That's it! Perfect!

That's much more like it, isn't it? That's where it belongs. Perfect.

PEGGY. What? Just there? Across the window?

JOHN. It makes sense. That way you'll get the light. See what you're doing.

PEGGY. No, but it spoils the view, doesn't it? I mean, sitting here I was enjoying the view. Just now, I could sit here and watch you coming up through the gate. Home from work. Now there'll be a desk in the way, won't there?

JOHN. Yes, but look at it this way – *(To the* **REMOVAL MEN.***)* – carry on, chaps, ignore her – look at it this way. You'll be sitting at your desk doing your household accounts in a perfectly good light, so there's no strain on your eyes and you can still glance up and see me coming through the gate just the same.

(The **REMOVAL MEN** *have left during the last.)*

PEGGY. I'd still like the sofa here. So long as we have curtains, that is.

JOHN. *(Doubtfully.)* Curtains in the daytime, it's going to get pretty dark in here, isn't it?

PEGGY. No. Net curtains.

JOHN. Net curtains?

PEGGY. *(Giggling.)* To stop people looking in at us getting up to no good on the sofa.

JOHN. Net curtains weren't part of the plan, were they?

PEGGY. Well, they jolly well ought to have been. Nobody can live without net curtains. Not in their front room, certainly. We always had net curtains, even during the blackout. Mummy insisted on them.

JOHN. Yes, I remember. They were extremely dusty.

PEGGY. I wouldn't feel safe without them. I mean, as a woman.

JOHN. Depends what you're planning to get up to in here, doesn't it?

PEGGY. *(Coyly, nuzzling him.)* Mmmm! You'd be surprised, Mr War Hero!

JOHN. Tally-ho! Come to think of it, wasn't this sofa also the scene of our other crime?

PEGGY. Other crime?

JOHN. Our second born? Young Richard? Wasn't Dickie also a child of this sofa?

PEGGY. Oh, no, he was upstairs. Dickie was assembled upstairs.

JOHN. Was he?

PEGGY. By then, we'd plucked up the courage – I'd plucked up the courage...

JOHN. Braved your snoring father.

PEGGY. I remember you said, "Oh, to hell with it, they must know what we're up to by now, surely?"

JOHN. Well, I think even they'd have put two and two together by then. We'd already presented them with a two-year-old granddaughter, for God's sake! Though I do seem to recall there was still a rather frosty atmosphere at breakfast the following morning, nonetheless. "What were you up to with my daughter last night?" "None of your business, old chap."

*(**PEGGY** giggles.)*

*(**SANDRA** returns from the hall still holding the phone, now disconnected again.)*

SANDRA. *(Grimly to herself.)* ... I know exactly where you are, you bugger... I could even hear the bloody jukebox in the background...

(She opens the dining room doors again. Voices as before though a couple of the girls appear to be crying.)

(Artificially brightly.) Here I am! Back at last –

(She pauses in the doorway and takes in the scene.)

(With a cry of horror.) Oh, my God, what the hell have you been doing in here? What's this all over the floor? Is this trifle? Dear God, it's all over the bloody walls, as well. It's everywhere! Jennifer, for Christ's sake, girl, I left you in charge, didn't I, you stupid creature? Go on, all of you! Out! Out! Out, every one of you! No, through the kitchen, you stupid boy don't you dare tread all that through here. Into the kitchen! Out!

(She goes inside and closes the doors behind her.)

*(As she does this, **JOHN** rises abruptly and moves to the centre of the room. He looks first at the sofa, then at the sideboard, then at the desk, then back at the sofa. He shakes his head. **PEGGY** watches him.)*

PEGGY. *(Anxiously.)* What's the problem? Is there a problem?

JOHN. I think we've got this sofa in the wrong place, as well.

PEGGY. Oh, no!

(**JOHN** *crosses swiftly to the door.*)

JOHN. *(Calling.)* I say, would you possibly come back in again for a moment?

PEGGY. How can it be in the wrong place? I thought we'd agreed...?

JOHN. *(Indicating the wall opposite the sideboard.)* It should be over there. I clearly remember, according to the plan, we put it there. It belongs over there.

PEGGY. It belongs here. It's perfectly happy here.

JOHN. Not according to the plan.

PEGGY. *(Mildly distressed.)* Well, bother the plan...

(The **REMOVAL MEN** *re-enter, manoeuvring a capacious armchair matching the sofa.)*

JOHN. Aha! Here's my armchair! Splendid! Sorry chaps, I'm going to have to ask you to move this sofa one more time. Just along that wall there. Would you mind, awfully?

(The **REMOVAL MEN** *drop the armchair in the centre of the room and move to shift the sofa once again.)*

(**PEGGY** *gets off it reluctantly. She is still sulking slightly.)*

PEGGY. *(As they do so.)* These poor men have been moving it backwards and forwards all afternoon. I'm so sorry. My husband's extremely particular.

JOHN. *(Laughing.)* If you hadn't been such a muddle head and mislaid the plan in the first place, darling... *(Shaking his head, to the* **REMOVAL MEN**, *laughing.)* Women, eh? What can you do with them? *(Watching them as they move it.)* That's it! That's more like it! Well done, chaps!

PEGGY. *(Muttering.)* It doesn't look right there! It really doesn't look at all happy, poor thing! Not at all!

JOHN. Ignore her. *(Indicating.)* Now, the armchair – my armchair – that belongs here, facing the sofa.

(The **REMOVAL MEN** *return to the armchair and position it during the next, according to his wishes.)*

PEGGY. *(As they do this.)* Your armchair? When did it suddenly become your armchair?

JOHN. I rather fancied it. Had my eye on it for some time. *(To the* **REMOVAL MEN**.*)* That's it! That's it! That'll do!

PEGGY. It used to be Daddy's armchair. He always sat in it. Until his legs went of course and he found he couldn't get out of it on his own. And he was far too heavy for Mummy to lift on her own...

JOHN. Yes, I've had my eye on it for a time... thanks, chaps! I think that's about it for this room. Just that small table to come and that's the lot.

(The **REMOVAL MEN** *leave.)*

(Seating himself into the chair.) Oh, yes! This'll do me nicely. Very comfy!

*(***PEGGY** *sits back in the middle of the sofa, looking somewhat isolated.)*

(A pause between them.)

*(***SANDRA** *backs out of the dining room, still with the phone, talking to someone behind her.)*

SANDRA. ...no, Justin, not this way! You go through there with the others! That way, through the kitchen. I'm not having you trampling that mess through here, not on this carpet... through the kitchen and into the garden now! Thank you! I have the feeling you were responsible for this, Justin Penfold! Yes, you might well smile, you little monster! I'm having a word with your father, Councillor Penfold about this! Go on! Off you go, you little horror.

(She closes the dining room doors, shutting out the diminishing sound as the children slowly depart. She crosses to the hall.)

(To herself, as she goes.) ...need to have the whole room redecorated... good mind to send them the bloody bill...

*(**SANDRA** goes out into the hall.)*

PEGGY. *(After a pause.)* No, it just doesn't feel right. I'll be sitting here staring at the sideboard.

JOHN. No you won't. You'll be staring at me.

PEGGY. You won't always be there, will you?

JOHN. Mostly. Whenever I'm home I will be. Staring back at you.

PEGGY. Oh. I see.

JOHN. What's the matter?

PEGGY. Be a bit lonely, won't it?

JOHN. Lonely?

PEGGY. *(Rather sulkily.)* Both on our separate chairs? All on my own on this great big sofa. Staring at the sideboard.

JOHN. You won't be on your own, you daft thing.

PEGGY. Won't I?

JOHN. You'll have the kids, won't you?

*(The **REMOVAL MEN** re-enter with the coffee table.)*

Ah, yes! Just put it there, between us. Thanks. That'll do.

*(**PEGGY** glumly surveys this new object that has somehow come between them.)*

PEGGY. *(Muted.)* Thank you.

*(The **REMOVAL MEN** depart.)*

JOHN. What's the matter?

PEGGY. *(Smiling to herself, wryly.)* Everything belongs where it belongs, doesn't it?

JOHN. *(Somewhat mystified.)* What? What are you talking about now?

PEGGY. I really ought to make them some tea, you know. I meant to offer them some earlier.

JOHN. I think they'd appreciate it. Thirsty work.

PEGGY. It's just we're running terribly low on tea. I'm terrified we'll run out. And I know how you love your early morning cup of tea in bed.

JOHN. You can always buy some more, can't you?

PEGGY. It's still rationed, John, tea's still rationed.

JOHN. God, is it? I'd no idea!

PEGGY. No, you wouldn't, why should you? You're a man. There's masses of things that are still rationed. You've no idea what it's like for us women.

JOHN. I thought we were over all that. For God's sake, it's 1952! The war's been over for ages! What else is still rationed, then?

PEGGY. Practically everything. Sugar. Bacon. Butter. Cheese...

JOHN. Oh, yes I knew cheese was still on the ration. I'd no idea about bacon, that's bad news...

PEGGY. ...margarine. Eggs. Cooking fat. Meat –

JOHN. Alright! Don't go on, darling, there's no need to go on...

PEGGY. It's ridiculous! I don't know what's the matter with this country? It's that wretched Labour government we've just had, I blame them entirely. Why on earth didn't we stick with Winston? He wouldn't have allowed this, would he?

JOHN. Now, keep calm! Keep calm, old thing! He's back! Winnie's back, now, isn't he? We voted him back, didn't we?

PEGGY. Thank goodness!

JOHN. It was just a glitch. That Labour government was a moment of madness. I honestly think we've seen the last of that lot. They've had their turn now. This isn't Russia, thank God.

PEGGY. I bet those Germans are drinking tea by the bucketful, I bet they are...

JOHN. I wouldn't be surprised. Probably made with acorns if it is...

PEGGY. As soon as these men have gone, when I've found where I've packed the kettle, I'll make us both a cup, if you like.

JOHN. That'd be nice.

PEGGY. I thought we'd all have supper together, when you've collected the kids. Our first meal together to christen our new house.

JOHN. That sounds wonderful. What are you planning to give us?

PEGGY. Well, I know it's a bit unimaginative of me but I thought, with the move and the disruption, we could finish up the spam fritters I made...

JOHN. *(Less enthused.)* Oh, jolly good...

PEGGY. I know it's a bit monotonous but they're the kids favourites, especially Dickie's. I think Dickie would actually be perfectly happy eating spam fritters every single day… Sandy's slightly less keen on them though. But then she's already beginning to worry about her weight, poor darling. Isn't that terrible? Eight years old and she's already beginning to fret about it. I mean, it's pressure from the other girls at school, it must be.

JOHN. Presumably. I don't think that sort of thing would ever bother Dickie.

PEGGY. Yes, I have to say he is certainly getting a little bit – rotund.

JOHN. Rotund?

PEGGY. Quite a little tummy on him, these days.

JOHN. Rubbish! He's a boy, isn't he? A growing boy? By the time he's fourteen, he'll have converted it to muscle. I was the same at his age. Same with all my family. Emaciated girls. Circular boys. Look at me now. Wouldn't call me fat, would you?

PEGGY. No, not in the slightest.

JOHN. Well, you tell young Sandra to snap out of it. Worrying about her figure at her age. For God's sake, who's she hoping to attract? Eight year old boys?

PEGGY. No, of course not. I don't think she's actually wanting to attract anyone just at present. I hope not, anyway. She can face all those problems later, can't she? Poor girl.

JOHN. Less of the 'poor girl'. What about the 'poor boy' she'll be lying in wait for later? I feel sorry for him, poor chap. It's Dickie we should be worried for. I mean, let's face it, all Sandy needs to do when she feels she's ready is get her hair done, paint her face, pull on a girdle and she'll flatten the first man who takes her fancy. You girls, you've got it made!

PEGGY. *(Declining to further this discussion.)* Yes. Anyway. Spam fritters it is.

JOHN. I'll drive over and pick them up in a minute. As soon as these chaps are out of our driveway.

PEGGY. I think Mother will really miss having the grandchildren there. She's grown really close to them, you know. I think really and truly, I know this is a dreadful thing to say but I think she's an infinitely better grandmother than she ever was a mother. I think it's probably the age she's at. When we were children she was still very young, of course. Far too busy having fun herself to bother about us girls. I hope I won't be like that. I hope I'll be a good mother.

JOHN. You are a good mother. You're a perfect mother. They're both very lucky children to have you. To have both of us, come to that.

PEGGY. Ah, but, these are still early days, aren't they?

JOHN. How do you mean?

PEGGY. As they get older, as they – mature, things get more difficult for a parent, they say. So I've read.

JOHN. Ah, well, you can't believe everything you read, can you?

PEGGY. I sometimes think, all those things I learnt at school, geometry and algebra – things like that – improper fractions – it would have been far more useful if they'd just taught us parenting. Certainly for us girls. You know, how to be a parent.

JOHN. I think, the general assumption is that parenting is on the whole an instinctive process for a woman whereas very few of them are born with a natural aptitude for algebra.

PEGGY. *(Unconvinced.)* Yes. It sort of doesn't make sense though, does it?

(A slight pause.)

JOHN. *(Who has rather lost interest in this.)* When we come, I'll drive straight into our garage...

PEGGY. What? *(Realising.)* Oh. So you can show them the magic door?

JOHN. They'll love it.

PEGGY. I'm sure it'll impress Dickie. I'm not so sure about Sandy.

JOHN. No, there's not an awful lot impresses her, does it? What did you do during the war, Daddy? I was in charge of this airfield, darling, looking after this whole squadron of fighter planes, making sure things went smoothly for the brave chaps who flew them. You mean you tidied up after them, Daddy, like Mummy does for us? *(He laughs.)* My dad the war hero, eh?

PEGGY. Well, you can hardly blame her after all she's been through, can you? Those constant air raids and rationing and continually running for cover, poor child. Permanently living on a knife edge. What's left to surprise her? She's barely had a childhood at all, has she? I mean, Dickie's young enough it hasn't affected him quite so much –

JOHN. He's a boy, he's more resilient.

PEGGY. I don't know about that. I think he lives in a dream world half the time. Most things simply wash over him. No, I think it's affected Sandra rather more than she lets on. She lost her best friend recently, you know. Diphtheria. Five years old...

JOHN. Yes, yes, yes, you've told me. But that was a few years ago now, wasn't it?

PEGGY. Sandy's never got over it. It really affected her...

JOHN. She should have got over it, by now, surely?

PEGGY. Some people don't, darling, they really don't. It stays with them mentally.

JOHN. Oh, come on, all this mental mumbo-jumbo, it's complete rubbish, most of the time... I mean, take that warehouse I'm working in at present. It's full of ex-service chaps claiming mental trauma which is just a damn good excuse to go behind the packing cases for a crafty smoke, if you ask me...

PEGGY. Darling, how can you say that?

JOHN. It's perfectly true, I mean come on, fair do's, we've all been through it, haven't we? Personally speaking, I lost dozens of my best chaps. I was deeply fond of many of them. Salt of the earth. Hardly a day went by without another crate reported missing. Whole flight crew sometimes. But in the end you just got on with it, didn't you. Cold bath, quick snifter, bite the bullet, carry on. That's the way most of us coped with it.

PEGGY. You're one of the lucky ones, darling, you're particularly strong and resilient.

JOHN. No, it's not just me. Take your father, for instance, he's a good example. During the first outing, fourteen to eighteen, he went through all that carnage in France, didn't he? From all accounts absolute hell on earth. But then he comes home, right as rain, never says a single word about it. Perfectly levelheaded, sanest man you could ever hope to meet. Bit on the dull side, if I'm entirely honest.

PEGGY. He was very strict when we were little, particularly at meal times, with me and my sisters. Especially my older sisters.

JOHN. Really? How strict was that?

PEGGY. Oh, you know. Elbows on the table, that sort of thing. Holding our knives and forks properly. He once stuck a broom handle down the back of my sister Melanie's dress to make her sit up properly. And as for leaving the table before everyone else had finished... Mealtimes were real nightmares. I used to suffer from dreadful indigestion.

JOHN. Pity he didn't instigate that for his grandchildren, if you ask me.

PEGGY. What for our two? Oh, surely not? You're joking?

JOHN. Dreadful table manners, both of them. The way Sandra slouches, she could do with an occasional broom handle...

PEGGY. Well. I'd far sooner you didn't. *(Hesitating.)* In fact, John... I do wish you wouldn't be quite so ready to...

JOHN. What? Ready to what?

PEGGY. Be ready to – smack them quite so often as you do. Ever since you've been home you... I've been meaning to say for some time.

JOHN. *(Rather coolly.)* Have you now? You're questioning how I choose to bring up our children now, are you?

PEGGY. No, not really, I just feel sometimes you...

JOHN. How I choose to bring up our children, darling, is my concern. As their father, as the man of the house, I'm ultimately responsible for discipline. It's the way my father brought me up and I have to say, that a good firm slap, now and again or, when necessary, something stronger, never did me the slightest harm. Indeed I like to think it made me the man I am.

> *(**PEGGY** blinks, considers a response but then thinks better of it. Instead she moves to the door.)*

PEGGY. I'll – see how those men are getting on. They must be nearly finished by now. Then I must start on the kitchen. It's chaos in there. They've just left everything strewn everywhere.

JOHN. I'll leave that entirely to you, darling. You're o/c culinary department on this station. Don't want to get under your feet, do I?

*(**PEGGY** goes out.)*

*(**JOHN** closes his eyes and sits back comfortably.)*

Hmmm! This is nice! Home sweet home.

(After a moment, from the hall a phone rings.)

*(**JOHN** remains oblivious. In a moment, he picks up his evening paper and starts to read it.)*

(The ringing continues.)

*(**SANDRA** eventually sticks her head out of the dining room to check she has heard it. Since we last saw her, she has donned a pair of gloves, headscarf and an apron. Holding a mop, she is clearly in the process of repairing the damage recently done to the dining room. She makes her way out to the hall to answer the phone.)*

*(**JOHN** reads on.)*

(The lights change to a third state, this time we are in 2022. It is a late November morning and bright sunlight shines through the blinds, currently at the front window.

Accompanying this change, comes a burst of pre-recorded music.)*

(Despite the passing of time, the room is identically furnished and much the same with the exception of a third door which has recently been knocked through to accommodate an extension ground floor study in place of the original garage. Once again, this new doorway only exists for the current occupants, **ALISON** *and* **JESS** *who, as will soon become apparent, are in the process of moving out.)*

*(***JESS***, in her late thirties, now enters from this most recent doorway. She is carrying a large cardboard box filled with office stuff.)*

JESS. *(Calling behind her.)* Sure you're done with all this lot? They're not due here till midday. There's no mad rush...

(She goes out into the hall with the box.)

(The lights change back to 1952 as the music cuts off. **JOHN** *reads on in silence.)*

(After a moment, **PEGGY** *comes on from the hall, carefully carrying a cup of tea and clutching a coaster in the other hand.)*

PEGGY. *(As she enters.)* Mustn't spill this on our new carpet, must I? Here you are, darling. Something to warm your insides, before you brave the cold again.

JOHN. *(Without looking up.)* Lovely, thank you, darling...

---

* A licence to produce FAMILY ALBUM does not include a performance licence for any third-party or copyrighted music. Licensees should create an original composition or use music in the public domain. For further information, please see the Music and Third-Party Materials Use Note on page iii.

(She carefully places the coaster, then the cup and saucer on the table.)

PEGGY. I'll leave it here for you. It's chaos in the kitchen. I'm going to be up half the night sorting it out...

JOHN. *(Still engrossed in his paper.)* Oh, there's no need for that, surely? Wait till morning, can't it?

PEGGY. It can't possibly wait. What about breakfast? We'll all need something, won't we? The children will need something. They can't go to school on empty tummies, can they? And you'll need something too, won't you? You'll certainly need something. I may even have a little piece of bacon left, I'm not promising...

JOHN. Oh, bravo, bravo, my little hero...

(She hurries out again.)

(He sits and continues to read, taking the occasional sip of tea.)

*(**SANDRA** returns from the hall with her phone. The lights change as she slowly makes her way as she talks back to the dining room.)*

SANDRA. *(As she enters, dryly.)* ...thank you so much for ringing back, anyway... no, I guessed that was where you must be... oh, were you? Were you indeed? Well, I have to say... I'm amazed, I never thought you had the slightest interest in all that... darling, you've been sports master there for seven whole years and this is the first year you've shown the remotest interest in the school Shakespeare production... which one is it this year? *Measure For Measure*. What fun! I wonder what's provoked your sudden interest? I suppose it has nothing to do with the exciting new young drama teacher, has it? What's her name? Glynis?... Miss Williams. I beg her pardon. How melodic, Glynis Williams!... Is she there with you? Only I thought I heard tinkling Welsh laughter over the jukebox... yes, by all means carry on, dearest, you can give her one or two notes... so much more important than your daughter's birthday party... Good luck with the production. You will remember though with that particular play, if I recall, it didn't end up at all happily for anyone, did it?

(She goes back into the dining room, closing the door.)

(Scarcely has she gone when the lights change again, the music returns * *and* **JESS** *enters from the hall with a mug of coffee and a couple of biscuits on a tray. She goes straight to the study door.)*

JESS. *(As she enters.)* Here you are! Keep you going.

ALISON. *(Offstage.)* Oh! Bless you, bless you, bless you...

(The lights change back to 1992. The music stops. There is a loud crash of breaking crockery from the dining room.)

SANDRA. *(Offstage, despairingly, from the dining room.)* Oh, shit! Oh fuck! Oh, bugger!

(**PEGGY** *comes in from the hall.)*

PEGGY. Finished with your cup, darling?

JOHN. Yes, thank you. Very nice, darling.

(She gathers up his cup, noticing he has failed to replace it on her carefully positioned coaster.)

---

* A licence to produce FAMILY ALBUM does not include a performance licence for any third-party or copyrighted music. Licensees should create an original composition or use music in the public domain.. For further information, please see the Music and Third-Party Materials Use Note on page iii.

PEGGY. *(Gently admonishing.)* Darling!

JOHN. What's that?

PEGGY. Careful with your cup. Mustn't mark the table, must we?

JOHN. *(Unconcerned.)* Oh, no. Sorry, darling.

*(**PEGGY** starts to return to the hall with the cup.)*

(Another crash from the dining room.)

SANDRA. *(Offstage.)* Oh, bollocks! Bollocks! Bollocks!

JOHN. Just reading here – spot of good news for you – the government are apparently planning to abolish tea rationing later on in the year...

PEGGY. Oh, good. That's wonderful news! *(Slight pause.)* Darling...

JOHN. Mmm?

PEGGY. Nearly time to collect the children...

JOHN. Yes, yes, yes. In a minute. One minute, darling. Just finish this.

*(**PEGGY** tiptoes out again.)*

*(**JESS** enters from the study.)*

(The lights change and the music returns.)*

(This time she crosses to the dining room.)

JESS. *(As she goes, issuing a command.)* Norman! Stop playing!

---

* A licence to produce FAMILY ALBUM does not include a performance licence for any third-party or copyrighted music. Licensees should create an original composition or use music in the public domain.. For further information, please see the Music and Third-Party Materials Use Note on page iii.

(There is a beep and the music stops abruptly. She has a sudden thought and pauses briefly at the sideboard to open a drawer.)

(Surveying the contents.) Damn!

(As she does this, the 1992 front door bell rings.)

(**SANDRA** *comes hurrying out of the dining room and goes to the front door. She is still in her cleaning mode. The door bell rings again.)*

SANDRA. *(As she crosses, rather flustered.)* Just a minute! Just a fucking minute!

(**JESS** *has closed the drawer and goes off into the dining room.)*

(**SANDRA** *returns almost immediately.)*

(Calling back to the hall.) ...no, they've all had a marvellous time. Ali was so thrilled your two could make it, Janice. They're playing in the garden at the moment. It's such a lovely day. *(Fiercely stopping them.)* NO, PLEASE, NOT THIS WAY! Straight down the hall through the kitchen and then follow the noise... you'll have to excuse me, I'm just doing a spot of mopping up... *(As she hurries back to the dining room, to herself.)* After your sodding children, as it happens...

(She goes back into the dining room. **PEGGY** *appears in the hall doorway again.)*

PEGGY. Darling...

JOHN. Hmm?

PEGGY. The men have finished unloading. They're just off.

JOHN. Right-o.

PEGGY. Only they can't get out. They say would you move the car.

JOHN. *(Mildly irritated.)* Oh, for heaven sake! *(He rises.)*

PEGGY. I think it might be starting to snow. Do you think we ought to tip them?

JOHN. Yes, of course we need to tip them...

PEGGY. Only I'm afraid I'm running terribly low on housekeeping his week, what with the move and stocking up and so on...

JOHN. Yes, I'll deal with it, darling, don't worry, I'll deal with it. Don't fuss, don't panic...

(He goes out into the hall.)

(She hesitates, then hurries to the table to inspect what damage he has caused with his cup. She rubs the mark with her fingers.)

(The 1992 doorbell rings again.)

(The dining room door opens and **SANDRA** *enters again and crosses to the front door.)*

PEGGY. *(Giving up on the mark.)* Oh, dear, oh, dear, oh dear...

(She hurries back through the hall door.)

SANDRA. *(Calling back.)* ...no, they're all out playing in the garden... *(Fiercely.)* NO, NOT THIS WAY! *(More reasonably.)* Straight down the hall through the kitchen and then follow the noise... *(Under her breath.)* Stupid woman!

(She returns to the dining room.)

*(***ALISON***, a woman of forty, enters from the study, sipping her mug of tea. She is*

deep in thought, working her mobile phone, apparently taking a brief break from her work. She sits at the desk and plonks her mug down on the surface.)

*(***PEGGY*** returns from the hall clasping a duster and a small tin of furniture polish.)*

(In due course she sets about repairing the table.)

(The 1992 doorbell rings again. **SANDRA** *again hurries out from the dining room to the hall.)*

(The doorbell rings twice again.)

(As she crosses.) ALRIGHT! ALRIGHT! ALRIGHT!

(She goes out into the hall.)

*(***JESS*** comes out of the dining room with a cardboard box. She crosses to the sideboard and opens the drawer again.)*

JESS. Nearly forgot to pack the cutlery, didn't we?

ALISON. Ah.

JESS. You OK?

ALISON. Just taking a break.

JESS. I thought you said it was a rush job?

(She starts to off-load the assorted contents of the cutlery drawer into the box.)

ALISON. It is a rush job. I've got the mother of a splitting headache coming on, that's all.

JESS. I'm not surprised, you've been at it since dawn, haven't you? You know what the doctor said. Regular breaks from your screen, every couple of hours...

ALISON. What do you think I'm doing now?

JESS. You've been at it more than a couple of hours You need to take care of yourself, Ali darling, you really do. All we need is for your health to break down and God help both of us...

ALISON. We'll just have to live off your earnings, won't we?

(The 1992 doorbell rings again.)

JESS. *(Amused.)* Mine? If we're reduced to depending on my BBC pittance, be prepared for a slump in the standard of living, that's all I can say. You can wave goodbye to the new house that's for certain.

(The 1992 doorbell rings yet again.)

(Examining the cutlery.) You know, some of this stuff I've never seen before, I don't think we've ever used half of it, have we? Not in all the time we've been here?

(The doorbell rings a third time.)

(This time an extremely irritated **SANDRA** *emerges.)*

SANDRA. *(Yelling.)* Jennifer! Jennifer! Answer the bloody door! I told you to answer the fucking door, child!

(The doorbell rings again.)

(Hurrying to the front door.) Useless, useless girl! I'm not paying her! I refuse to pay her...

(She goes out.)

JESS. *(Holding up a bone handled table knife.)* Where'd this come from, for instance? *(Holding up an equivalent fork.)* And this?

ALISON. I think they're a left over from my parents. Or possibly even my grandparents. Where did you find them? In the drawer?

JESS. Oh, well who needs knives and forks, when you have perfectly good fingers?

ALISON. Perfectly adequate for takeaway.

JESS. Come to that, when was the last time we ever ate a meal off that bloody great table in there? Far too busy building expensive extensions, weren't we?

ALISON. I needed my workspace. We weren't using the garage anyway, were we?

JESS. Who needs a car in London these days?

(She holds up a large carving fork.)

Right. Three guesses as to what this is?

ALISON. That, my dear working class oik, is a good old-fashioned, middle-class carving fork.

JESS. *(Blankly.)* Carving fork?

ALISON. Which, together with a carving knife made up a carving set which formed a central part of the ritual, observed by every self-respecting middle-class family, generally at Sunday lunchtime.

JESS. Ah, I see. Religious, was it?

ALISON. Oh, no, far from it. This is England, darling. Strictly gastronomic.

JESS. Oh, I see. It wasn't used for sacrificing the children, then?

ALISON. God, no, otherwise knowing my beloved father, my brothers and I wouldn't have survived beyond the age of five. No this ritual was known as 'The Carving of the Sunday Roast', in which the father would stand at the head of the table, studying the joint of meat which mother had spent the last three hours single-handedly preparing but who now sat meekly with her children, head bowed as father, like some mediaeval blacksmith, dexterously drew the carving knife swiftly backwards and forwards across the steel sharpener with the mighty sound of whistling and grinding, rendering the knife even blunter than it was before...

JESS. My God, that must have been exciting! You middle classes knew how to live it up... it were never like that in Heckmondwike...

ALISON. ...and then, at the climax – wait, we haven't yet reached the climax – the master of the house, satisfied that he had honed his blade to its razor sharp peak, then sets about the joint of meat with knife and fork, both hands working in synchronised perfection, carving mysteriously uneven triangular chunks of meat of varying thickness which he then distributes at random to his starving family who are now sat desperate to help themselves to the stone cold vegetables which have been standing on the table for the past two hours.

JESS. So who was this master carver, then? Your granddad, was it?

ALISON. No, my dad. At least while he was still around. Till he left us and buggered off with his Welsh drama teacher. No, my granddad's carving days were over by then. We only saw him once a month, if that. Whenever we went to visit him in the care home.

JESS. Were you fond of him?

ALISON. Not very. He was a bad tempered old man, who never remembered my name, and was always telling me to stand up straight.

JESS. I was very fond of my granddad. He was great. We used to go fishing together.

ALISON. That must have been fun.

JESS. It was. *(Smiling.)* He used to make me laugh a lot, did granddad. *(Returning to the carving fork.)* Well, I must say in all my childhood I never saw one of these, lass. My granddad had no use for one of these.

ALISON. Except for spearing fish perhaps?

JESS. He weren't a bloody eskimo.

ALISON. But then you did come from a terribly deprived background, didn't you? You'd find it hard to pick up your mushy peas and faggots with that, wouldn't you?

JESS. That's enough! I propose that this carving fork has no place in a self-respecting vegetarian household and that we bin it forthwith.

ALISON. Seconded.

JESS. Unless, do you think, it could be an antique? In which case it might be worth a few bob, mightn't it? I might manage to sell it to some old age pensioner, still pining for his Sunday roast.

(She drops the fork into the box with the other items which she takes into the dining room.)

ALISON. Preferably one with any teeth left. I'd better get on. I need to finish this before I pack things away. *(Calling.)* What time are they due, by the way?

JESS. *(Returning.)* Any minute now. I'd better call in case they're running late. They did warn me they had an earlier job. Have you a lot left to do?

ALISON. Half an hour's worth, if that. Give me a yell when they're here...

(She goes back to her study.)

*(**JESS** checks to see the drawer is finally empty.)*

(She notices **ALISON** *has left her coffee mug on the desk and goes to retrieve it. She then stops and lingers, staring out of the window.)*

*(***PEGGY*** enters holding a duster and a tin of furniture polish. She is flushed and excited at the prospect of bringing a sense of order to their new home. She stands in the middle of the room surveying it.)*

*(***SANDRA*** backs out of the dining room, clutching the mop and talking to someone in the room behind her.)*

SANDRA. *(To someone in the room.)* ...don't give me all that fucking "boys will be boys" nonsense, Gordon Penfold, look what your Neanderthal son has done to my wallpaper, you smug Tory arsehole...

(The invisible party has clearly left the dining room via the hall.)

*(***SANDRA***, anticipating his intentions, dashes across the living room and out into the hall still clutching the mop.)*

(As she crosses.) Oh, no you bloody don't! No you don't...

*(***PEGGY*** still stands happily surveying her new room.)*

PEGGY. *(Happily, looking around her.)* So much to do... so much to do...

(From the direction of the hall, presumably through the open front door, the sound of screams, breaking glass and a car alarm. **SANDRA** *returns, holding her mop which she has clearly used as an offensive weapon. She*

crosses to the dining room doors and throws it inside the room. As she does this, the sound of a **GIRL**'s *voice from the hall.)*

GIRL. *(Offstage, plaintively.)* Mummy, how could you? That was his car! How could you? How could you do that to his car?

SANDRA. *(As she enters.)* Oh, do shut up, Alison, you wimp! It's only a bloody car, for God's sake!

(From the hall, the **GIRL** *bursts into tears and is heard running upstairs.)*

(Swaying slightly.) Christ, I'm completely knackered!

(She flings herself full length on the sofa.)

PEGGY. Now then, where to start?

(Her gaze alights on the sideboard. She sets to with her duster and polish.)

SANDRA. *(From the sofa, eyes closed, wearily.)* Never again! Never, never, never again!

JESS. *(Still at the window, to herself.)* Funny. I'll rather miss this place...

(As she continues to stare out, **SANDRA** *dozes, and* **PEGGY** *polishes with gusto, the lights fade to a...)*

(Blackout.)

End of Act One

ACT TWO

(The same.)

(In all cases, time has moved forward.)

(In 1952, it is now a few days later. **JOHN** *and* **PEGGY** *and their two children* **SANDRA** *and* **RICHARD** *(***SANDY** *and* **DICKIE***) have now moved in and settled into a steady routine.)*

(In 1992, it is a few months later, late autumn. Time enough to have marked **SANDRA***'s considerable deterioration over a few weeks.)*

(In 2022, where the action begins, it is only an hour or so later and the same bright November morning. **JESS** *and* **ALISON** *are still awaiting the arrival of the removal men.* **ALISON** *is sitting on the sofa, surrounded by work papers, whilst* **JESS** *anxiously paces about.)*

(A silence between them.)

ALISON. *(Slightly accusatory.)* Well, how long are they going to be, these people? Did they even say a time?

JESS. *(Unhappily.)* He said sometime early afternoon. Two-ish probably. Two thirty at worst.

ALISON. There's a hell of a difference between that and eleven a.m.

JESS. *(Miserably.)* Yes, I know. Sorry.

ALISON. Not your fault. Not entirely.

JESS. *(At the window.)* It's a beautiful day. They can't blame it on the weather.

ALISON. How did you find them in the first place, this removal firm?

JESS. They were on the online notice board.

ALISON. What notice board?

JESS. At the BBC.

ALISON. *(Faintly incredulous.)* You got them off a BBC notice board?

JESS. Yes, they also came highly recommended by this producer I was working with.

ALISON. Who was that?

JESS. Diana. Diana Teal.

ALISON. Oh, her. The one with all the teeth. The one that does the documentaries? Archaeology?

JESS. Right. She and her partner recently moved house and I mentioned we were also on the move and she recommended them. Apparently there are very few decent removal firms left these days. Since the best of them left and went back to mainland Europe.

ALISON. Come back Carter Paterson, all is forgiven. What's happening to this bloody country, it's spiralling ever downwards. What are they called, anyway? Do they even have a name, this firm?

JESS. *(Hesitantly.)* They're called – well, they call themselves 'Up Yours'. I know, I know, they don't sound at all promising, but Diana said don't be put off by that and she swore by them...

ALISON. Let me get this straight. You are entrusting thousands of pounds worth of my precious technical gear to an outfit called 'Up Yours'?

JESS. Sorry. I didn't mention the name, just in case...

ALISON. I think I'd have seen it, wouldn't I, the moment their van arrived with 'Up Yours' painted on the side? That's presuming they even own a van and don't arrive with the handcart?

JESS. Oh, yes, there's a van. There's definitely a van. Bright yellow.

ALISON. Bright yellow.

JESS. I'll give them another call in a minute.

(In 1952, it is now early spring and the sun is shining on a Saturday afternoon. The lights change briefly to reflect this. **PEGGY** *enters from the hall and crosses to the window. She looks out evidently waiting for someone to arrive.)*

You sit there and make yourself comfortable. Put your feet up if you like.

ALISON. I don't know about comfortable, not on this thing. It's agony to sit on. Full of weird lumps. Mind you, it does have a distinguished history. Family rumour has it that my mother, during a night of furtive wartime passion in her parents' house, was actually conceived on this very sofa.

JESS. You should put up a plaque.

ALISON. I'd forgotten how uncomfortable it was. We've rarely used this room of late, have we?

JESS. Not since we had the conservatory put on at the back. I can't remember ever sitting in here. I've always considered this room part of the Stanton Museum. I even considered putting ropes round it at one time.

(**ALISON** *shifts uncomfortably.)*

If it's that uncomfortable, why don't you sit on the chair?

ALISON. Oh, no, no, no, I couldn't possibly! That chair's sacrosanct. That is strictly a male preserve. We knew it as Grandfather's Throne upon which, according to my mother, he ruled supreme and unquestioned. Totally destroying his family's lives in the process.

JESS. And presumably your father continued the tradition?

ALISON. I've no doubt he would have done. Only he was never here long enough to actually sit on the thing, was he?

JESS. It's safe to stand here, is it?

ALISON. Probably not. I tell you, there isn't a square foot in this room where some luckless child at some time or another hasn't wet themselves with fear.

JESS. Including you, I take it?

ALISON. Including me. Mainly watching my mother fall apart before my eyes.

JESS. I presume we won't be taking the chair with us either, then? No. *(Reflecting, with a smile.)* Me and my brother, we nearly came to blows over who should have granddad's rocker, I remember.

ALISON. Who got it in the end, you sentimental Northern soul?

JESS. He did. He was bigger than me.

*(**PEGGY** goes out again to the hall.)*

(The lights revert back.)

*(**JESS** continues to wait restlessly by the window.)*

Got everything switched off in there, have you?

ALISON. All switched off and stowed away. I warn you, though I fully intend to travel with it in the van. I'm not trusting this lot. Some of that stuff's irreplaceable.

JESS. No, I've already said, I'll travel in the van. You can take a taxi.

ALISON. No, you're taking the taxi. I'm in the van. *(Firmly.)* No arguments. Final.

JESS. *(Happy to concede.)* Okay, if you're happy with that. I know you can't wait to leave this place, but –

ALISON. Can't wait.

JESS. – but I was thinking you know, the other day, I'll be rather sorry to leave here, you know.

ALISON. Will you?

JESS. I'm going to have to acclimatise. Get used to living north of the river. I've grown quite fond of this place over the years. Got used to all its historical quirks and peculiarities. Won't you? Even a little?

ALISON. Won't I what?

JESS. Miss it?

ALISON. No. Not at all.

JESS. It's your family home, though. Doesn't it feel odd, finally moving out?

ALISON. Why should it?

JESS. Not the slightest?

ALISON. It's just a house. A haunted house.

JESS. All your childhood images? Memories of growing up?

ALISON. I can hardly remember most of them. I tried to put them out of my mind.

JESS. I can remember things from my childhood like they were yesterday.

ALISON. Fishing with your granddad?

JESS. *(Smiling.)* Yes. That and other things. My mum in the kitchen making pastry...

ALISON. *(Closing her eyes and wincing.)* Dear God, Jess! I'd no idea I'd gone and married a 1930s picture postcard. Was the family dog in the corner eagerly wagging its tail?

(In 1992, it is autumn in the midst of a late summer storm.)

*(**SANDRA** enters rapidly through the hall doorway, having recently shed her coat in the hall. She holds the usual phone. As she does so, there is a rumble of thunder from outside and a quick splatter of rain on the window pane. She drops the phone on the desk and crosses up and goes out through the dining room doors for a moment.)*

JESS. *(A sudden thought.)* Hey, I just remembered. You say you've put it all out of your mind. What about all those Sunday dinners, then? You remembered those, didn't you?

ALISON. I'd prefer not to have done. They're another set of bad dreams.

JESS. God, that is so sad. I am sorry. If I'd known you felt like that about the place I'd never have agreed to move in with you. I mean, if you felt it was haunted, if it's given you such bad feelings all these years...

ALISON. No, as I say, I've suppressed them mostly. It's only recently – I suppose with the move, it's all come flooding back...

JESS. ... I mean we didn't have to stay here, did we? We could have found somewhere else, surely?

ALISON. Be honest, we didn't have an awful lot of choice at that stage of our lives, did we? Financially? It was only I'd recently inherited this place and it was just so – convenient, wasn't it? It's only now we're leaving... All the skeletons are suddenly jumping out of their cupboards.

JESS. I'm getting nervous to go upstairs again now...

(**SANDRA** *returns with a hand towel mopping her head and face from the rain. She sits at the desk. She picks up the phone, deliberating as to whether to make a call.)*

Funny, I've told you all about my childhood, haven't I? Gone on about it for ages, haven't I? You must be bored to death hearing about it.

ALISON. *(Affectionately.)* I love hearing about your childhood, Jess darling. I know I sometimes joke about it, but that's probably because I'm jealous. You always make it seem so uncomplicated and – innocent, somehow. Sorry, does that sound terribly patronising?

JESS. Yes, it does. It sounds extremely patronising...

ALISON. Yes, but yours was a happy childhood wasn't it, darling. It's left you with fond memories, ones you choose to remember, ones you're happy to share with others.

JESS. Well, I suppose I may have prettied it up, slightly. It's not to say we didn't have our moments. Hell, we had our moments. My mum had a real temper on her, I can tell you. When she was angry you learnt to duck, if you didn't want a clip round the ear. Why do you think I chose to live with you?

ALISON. *(Immediately defensive.)* What are you talking about? That's outrageous! I've never laid a finger on you...

JESS. Ah, but you've been known to throw things, haven't you?

ALISON. *(Reluctantly conceding.)* Yes, I admit I've thrown things. I've certainly thrown things. But never at you. I never intended to hit you with them.

JESS. Nonetheless you managed to, didn't you?

ALISON. Once. Once, purely by accident.

JESS. Once is enough.

ALISON. It was an accident. It was never meant to hit you, it bounced off something else! God, how many more times? What else do I have to do to apologise? I bought you dinner, a bottle of that prohibitively expensive champagne. I even bought you bloody flowers, didn't I? What more do you want?

*(**JESS** smiles enigmatically.)*

*(During the next, **SANDRA** comes to a decision and punches a number into her phone.)*

(Suspiciously.) You're just bringing this up to get back at me, aren't you? Because I made you feel guilty for cocking things up with this removal firm? That's why you've brought all this up again, isn't it? Yes it is!

JESS. *(Over-dramatically.)* It still hurts this shoulder. Where you hit it! *(A little shiver of pain.)* Aaah!

ALISON. Oh, piss off!

*(**SANDRA** gets a reply on her phone which has gone to answer.)*

SANDRA. *(Irritated.)* Oh, not again! *(Into phone.)* Hello, Dickie. It's big sister again. I'm sorry I keep getting your answering thing... sorry but I do badly need to talk to you, Dickie, things aren't good here... not at all. We had the most terrible row the other night, it woke up the whole house, it must have done. He's definitely gone this time. Sorry to keep bothering you and tying up your answering thing like this but I really don't know who else to talk to. Please, please, please, do call me back. Otherwise I'll try again later. 'bye.

(She disconnects.)

*(**JESS** has gone to sit beside **ALISON** on the sofa.)*

JESS. *(As she sits, reacting.)* God! I see what you mean about the lumps! *(Penitently.)* Sorry. I didn't mean to tease you. You're not a bully. Not at all. You're the gentlest person I know. I love you really.

(She kisses her partner gently on the forehead.)

ALISON. *(Smiling ruefully.)* I should be used to it. Being teased. My first memory was having life made unbearable being teased by my brothers. Especially Terry. He made my life hell. He sensed early on I was totally lacking in self-confidence. He delighted in telling me with a face like mine I'd never attract anyone, that sort of thing.

JESS. Bloody cheek! How dare he?

ALISON. Which at that age, of course, has you rushing neurotically to the nearest mirror.

JESS. How old were you when this was happening?

ALISON. Oh, I was at <u>that</u> age, you know. Old enough to start to have dreams but still young enough to have them shattered.

JESS. Didn't your parents try and stop him –?

ALISON. *(Laughing.)* My parents? Well, by that time my father was long gone, of course. And as for my mother, you'll have gathered she was hardly a pillar of strength at that stage. She needed all the support she could get.

JESS. Did she have the breakdown because of your father leaving?

ALISON. Partly that. And losing Eddie, of course.

JESS. Your younger brother?

ALISON. Eddie, yes. We grew quite close eventually, once he'd escaped from creepy Terry's shadow.

JESS. I can't say I took to Terry at all. On the one occasion we met.

ALISON. I'm amazed he even came to our wedding. Considering how strongly he disapproved. Practically the first thing he said to me was, "Hello, dear, still wasting your time drawing pretty pictures, are you?"

JESS. *(Rising impatiently.)* From the sound of it you lost the wrong brother, didn't you?

ALISON. Yep.

*(**SANDRA** has picked up the phone and is now punching in another number.)*

*(During the next, **JESS** sits in the armchair.)*

JESS. How old was he when he died?

ALISON. He was eighteen. Drug overdose. He was the one my God-fearing grandfather always referred to as Esau. Whereas smug big brother Terry, Terence Dickens QC, was most definitely Jacob, of course.

*(**SANDRA** gets a reply.)*

(She sighs again with exasperation.)

SANDRA. *(Into phone, brightly.)* Mummy?... It's me, Sandy. We keep missing each other, sorry. I badly need to talk to you. Do call me back again, won't you?

(She disconnects. Then sits trancelike throughout the following.)

ALISON. I was ten years old. Still at the local school here. One day, she didn't arrive to collect me. Which wasn't that unusual, of course. So I walked home on my own. When I got here I couldn't get a reply, so I let myself in with the key under the flowerpot and found her upstairs, lying on the bed unconscious. For a minute I thought she was dead.

JESS. Ten years old. What did you do?

ALISON. Eventually, when I couldn't wake her, I phoned for an ambulance. They came and took her straight in. Pumped out the remains of the painkillers. Kept her in observation for weeks.

JESS. What happened to you?

ALISON. Dear Daddy was forced to come and collect me, wasn't he? *(Smiling.)* Much to the Welsh diva's displeasure. She became convinced that I was trying to poison her. She became quite hysterical in the end...

JESS. Where on earth did she get that idea?

ALISON. Can't imagine. Possibly because I told her I was going to.

(A slight pause.)

*(**SANDRA** has started punching in another number on her phone.)*

Well, I was only ten.

JESS. I wouldn't put it past you if you had poisoned her.

SANDRA. *(Into phone.)* Hello, is that Mrs Cooper? This is Margaret Stanton's daughter, Sandy – Sandra Dickens... Peggy's daughter, yes... how clever of you to remember! ...oh, very well, thank you for asking. I was wondering, Mrs Cooper – Evette, yes – I've been trying to get in touch with my mother, only she doesn't appear to be answering her phone... within the last ten minutes or so... oh, yes? ...yes... yes, of course, how silly of me, to forget... you do lose all sense of time these days, don't you find? Yes... Yes I will... thank you so much if you'd be so kind, thank you. Goodbye.

(She disconnects.)

*(***JESS*** suddenly rises impatiently, taking her mobile from her pocket as she does so.)*

JESS. I'm sorry, this is getting ridiculous. I'm going to call these people. Tell them if they're not here in ten minutes I'm cancelling altogether...

(She moves to the dining room.)

ALISON. *(Mildly alarmed.)* No, for God's sake don't cancel them, Jess! If you cancel them, we'll never get away, will we?

*(***JESS*** has gone.)*

(Rising and moving back towards her study.) We'll be trapped in this bloody house for ever, otherwise...

*(***PEGGY*** comes in from the hall again.)*

(Again she looks out of the window anxiously.)

*(***ALISON*** goes off into her study.)*

PEGGY. *(To herself, anxiously.)* Golf! Golf! Golf! How long does it take to play a game of golf for goodness sake?

*(***PEGGY*** returns to the hall.)*

*(***SANDRA****'s phone rings.)*

(She answers immediately.)

(During the next, she rises and having meandered aimlessly, finishes up sitting on the sofa.)

SANDRA. *(Into phone.)* Hello, Mummy... thank you so much for calling back... did Mrs Cooper pass on my message? I suddenly remembered, of course, you do have lunch rather early there, don't you? ...Oh, did you? ...that sounds nice... broad beans or French beans? ...runner beans, right. Mummy, I do need to talk to you rather urgently because I'm feeling terribly low again... yes, the same as before, only a little bit worse. And I badly needed to talk to someone, that's all. And I know Daddy doesn't ever...he never wants to... talk about these sort of things, does he, but I just so needed to... *(Laughing.)* Yes, he'd probably tell me to go and have a cold bath, wouldn't he? ...Typical... what's that? ...No, no, the children are fine... they do miss Jeremy of course, but we've both agreed... certain weekends. She doesn't want them, of course. She wants nothing to do with them. Doesn't want them near her. Not that I'd ever let them within a mile, the poisonous little... what's that? ...Oh, did you? With custard, you say? That must have been delicious. Real custard, was it? ...No... not like you used to make, Mummy... but they're probably rushed off their feet there, aren't they? They simply don't have the hours in the day, poor things... Mummy, getting back to Jeremy, he's agreed to continue paying all the school fees and so on for the boys and then reasonable subsistence for me and Alison but I'm still finding it terribly hard to cope on my own, Mummy... I do need someone to help me. Anyone... all I'm asking is could you have a word with Daddy just to remind him he does have another child besides Dickie? ...What's that? ...No, it's me, Mummy... Sandra... Sandy... your daughter. Sandy... no, Mummy, I'm not Mrs Phillips... I don't even know Mrs Phillips... No... What? Oh it's time for your television programme, is it? ...No, no, you mustn't miss that, Mummy, don't miss it, will you? ...No... 'bye-'bye, now. Off you go!

(She rings off. In a moment, she slowly rises and, phone in hand, makes her way out of the hall door.)

(**JESS** *enters from the dining room with two fresh mugs of coffee.)*

JESS. *(Calling.)* They say they'll be here in five minutes. They're just turning into Tennyson Road.

ALISON. *(From the study, offstage.)* Hooray! Hooray!

JESS. To celebrate I've made us another cup of instant. You don't have to drink it, though.

(She goes into the study.)

(In 1952, **JOHN** *enters from the hall, flushed from his game of golf.)*

JOHN. *(Calling.)* Hello! Hello! Where is everyone?

(**PEGGY** *enters behind him.)*

PEGGY. Oh, there you are! I was wondering where you were.

JOHN. I told you, I was playing golf.

PEGGY. Yes, but you've been simply ages. You're not usually this long.

JOHN. No longer than usual.

PEGGY. Was it a specially difficult game?

JOHN. Difficult? What are you talking about, difficult? Golf's always difficult. That's the whole point of it. If it wasn't difficult, no one would bother playing it, would they?

PEGGY. No, I just thought you might have found it more difficult than usual with it taking you so long.

JOHN. Yes, well, I have to confess we did stop off at the nineteenth, one or two of us.

PEGGY. The nineteenth?

JOHN. For a quick snifter.

PEGGY. Who's us?

JOHN. One or two chaps from work.

PEGGY. What, the lazy ones?

JOHN. No, not them! They'd never survive the course! Senior management. That's who I was playing with.

PEGGY. Oh, I see. Senior management.

JOHN. Top brass. That's the way to get on, darling. Play 'em at their own game. And occasionally let 'em win. It's very quiet, where are the kids?

PEGGY. *(A little hesitantly.)* They're – they've gone round to play at granny and granddad's.

JOHN. What, on a Saturday?

PEGGY. Yes, I sent them round there.

JOHN. Why on earth did you do that? Didn't they mind?

PEGGY. Mind what?

JOHN. Your parents? Having the kids round there, disrupting their Saturday?

PEGGY. I just felt we both needed some time here. On our own. Without them.

JOHN. On our own? What are you talking about? Sex? Are you talking about sex? Are you wanting sex?

PEGGY. No, no, not sex. I certainly don't want sex. *(Hastily.)* I mean, no, not now, I mean. I do want it. I mean if you want the truth, I mean I'm in quite urgent need of it. But not just this minute.

JOHN. *(Laughing with relief.)* Thank God for that! I'm absolutely whacked.

PEGGY. No, I – I thought we needed to talk.

JOHN. Talk?

PEGGY. About – personal matters.

JOHN. Personal –? Oh, you mean sex? You want to talk about sex, do you?

PEGGY. No, John, please, I don't even want to talk about sex. Please leave sex entirely out of it. I need to talk about the children. It's the children I need to talk about.

JOHN. The children?

PEGGY. Yes.

JOHN. *(Sitting himself in his chair.)* Okay. What about them? Fire ahead. I'm listening.

*(**PEGGY** flaps about, an anxious supplicant, but eventually plucks up courage and sits on the sofa.)*

*(**JESS** comes out of the study and checks the window.)*

JESS. *(Calling back.)* Yes, it's them. Bright yellow van, big red letters, 'Up Yours'.

ALISON. *(Offstage, calling.)* That'll impress the neighbours...

(The 2022 doorbell rings.)

*(**JESS** goes off to the hall to answer it.)*

JOHN. Come on then, out with it. I'm listening.

JESS. *(Offstage, after a moment.)* Hello, there, do come in. Would you mind starting upstairs, please?

PEGGY. It's – it's to do with Sandy, really. She's doing frightfully well at school. Her teacher tells me she's streets ahead of the rest of her class.

JOHN. Yes, she's a bright girl. I saw her report. Doing a damn sight better than her wretched brother. But he's younger, of course. And he's a boy. He'll catch up. I have a feeling he may well surprise us all.

PEGGY. Yes, but staying with Sandy just for a moment. I just feel we've made no plans at all for her, have we?

JOHN. How do you mean, plans? What sort of plans?

PEGGY. For her future. Plans beyond that little local school she's currently at.

JOHN. Perfectly good school. Best in the district. We looked it up.

PEGGY. No, I'm talking about further education, higher education. With a brain like hers she deserves to go further, doesn't she? I mean maybe even, who knows, to university even?

JOHN. *(Faintly incredulous.)* University?

PEGGY. Why not? She's worth it! You've said yourself, she's a bright girl!

JOHN. Oh, no, no, no, no! Out of the question, darling! Totally out of the question!

PEGGY. Why? Why should it be out of the question?

JOHN. Because at the end of it, let's face it, she'll leave university, having cost us a small fortune, she'll promptly get a job in *Woolworths* and marry the first good-looking chap to walk in and buy a Mars bar. Complete waste of time and money.

*(**SANDRA** enters through the hall door. She is lurching somewhat and clearly very drunk.)*

Peggy?

(She weaves her way uncertainly to the dining room doors and goes out again.)

Darling?

(From the dining room there is a very loud crash as she falls over.)

Is that all you wanted to talk about? Just Sandy?

SANDRA. *(Offstage, from the dining room, with a cry.)* Shit!

(A **YOUNG GIRL***'s voice is heard, also from the dining room, very concerned.)*

GIRL. *(Offstage.)* Mummy! Mummy, are you alright?

SANDRA. *(Offstage, slightly slurred.)* I'm alright, darling, Mummy's alright...

GIRL. *(Offstage.)* Have you hurt yourself?

SANDRA. *(Offstage.)* No, I'm fine. Help me up, help me out, Ali darling. Be a good girl now and help Mummy up to bed...

JOHN. Peggy? Darling? Was that all? Was there anything else?

PEGGY. No. *(Slight pause.)* No, not really.

JOHN. I sense there was something. What is it?

PEGGY. *(Reluctantly.)* It just seems so terribly unfair, somehow...

JOHN. Unfair? How is it unfair?

PEGGY. We never seem to talk about Dickie like that, do we? Just simply dismiss him like that?

JOHN. Dickie's entirely different. He's a boy, for one thing. He'll have the sense not to get side-tracked. He'll have more sense than that.

PEGGY. Even though he's only half as bright as his sister?

JOHN. *(Rising impatiently.)* I'm sorry, I can't see where all this is leading, Margaret, I really can't. Currently, as things stand, we simply don't have money to burn, old love. Certainly not enough to waste on Sandy, however well-intentioned. *(Moving to the door.)* I'm going to have a bath. Water's still hot, I take it?

PEGGY. *(Muted.)* Yes, it should be.

JOHN. By the time I've had my bath, I'll have got my breath back, with any luck. If you still fancy a spot of rumpy-pumpy.

(He laughs.)

(She manages a faint smile in response.)

(Sensing she is still unhappy.) Cheer up, darling! You mustn't worry about the girl, you really mustn't. You've seen how happy she is up there in her room, playing with her dollies. Let nature take its course. Leave her to have her babies, for heaven's sake.

(He goes off through the hall.)

*(***PEGGY*** is left looking troubled.)*

PEGGY. *(Softly, to herself.)* She's special. I know she is. She's special.

*(***ALISON*** emerges from the study to watch the loading process from the window, sipping the remains of her coffee.)*

*(***JESS*** appears in the hall doorway.)*

ALISON. They appear to be getting on with it, anyway.

JESS. They seem fairly organised on the whole. Quick and efficient. I'm impressed. I told them to start upstairs with the things we're –

(From the hall a loud crash as something is dropped.)

ALISON. *(Reacting.)* Jesus!

JESS. Whoops! Spoke too soon!

ALISON. What was it?

JESS. *(Checking the hall behind her.)* Bedside light.

ALISON. Yours or mine?

JESS. Yours from the look of it.

ALISON. Good. I never cared for it.

JESS. I'm getting them to load the things we definitely need in the new place first. Most of it down here we agreed we're offloading to the store, haven't we?

ALISON. *(Surveying the room, critically.)* I can't see us wanting any of this, can you? Might as well try and sell it, if anyone wants it. It's either that or the tip.

JESS. You sure you don't want to keep any of it? Not even grandfather's throne? Seems a shame. Absolutely positive? Last chance to save the family history...

*(**ALISON** gives her a look and then moves to the dining room with her mug.)*

No, right. Get rid of the lot, then!

(As she goes out, calling.) As soon as you've finished up there, can you make a start in the kitchen, please...?

(She goes out.)

ALISON. *(In the doorway, calling after her.)* And we can lose this monstrosity in the dining room, as well. This table can certainly go. I've never liked it. We've bought a perfectly good new one, we might as well use it. *(With a final look round the living room.)* No, get rid of the lot of it.

(She goes off into the dining room.)

*(**PEGGY** rises from the sofa, still in a dream of her own, and crosses to the sideboard.)*

(She opens a drawer and takes out a duster and a tin of furniture polish. She starts, more by way of therapy than anything, to slowly polish the sideboard.)

(Slight pause.)

(From the hall, a ten-year-old girl's voice is heard calling:)

GIRL. *(Offstage, calling.)* Mummy? Mummy? Are you home? Mummy! Are you upstairs? *(Her voice receding as she climb the stairs.)* Mummy...? Mummy...? Mummy...?

PEGGY. *(Polishing, still in her own world.)* No, he's wrong. She's worth more than that! Far, far more...

(She completes her polishing and steps back to admire her handiwork.)

That's better! *(To the sideboard.)* You haven't had a proper polish for ages, have you?

(She moves to the hall doorway.)

(Pausing, with a final look of approval.) Yes!

*(**PEGGY** goes out into the hall.)*

*(**ALISON** comes out of the dining room and crosses straight to her study. She returns almost immediately pulling a large flight case presumably filled with her gear. She parks it by the desk in front of the window. She goes back into the study.)*

(She returns with a second flight case, this one is apparently much heavier.)

ALISON. *(Straining with the effort.)* Wooo!

(She parks this second case next to the first one. During this last manoeuvre, **JESS** *has entered to witness this.)*

JESS. Hey! Hey! Hey! You shouldn't be doing that on your own, you know.

ALISON. Oh, no?

JESS. Moving heavy weights like that. It can seriously damage your chances of children…

ALISON. Oh, good! Is that a promise?

JESS. Have you got everything just in those two cases?

ALISON. Yes.

JESS. What, absolutely everything?

ALISON. Apart from the desk, yes.

JESS. That's incredible.

ALISON. Depends how you pack it in the first place, doesn't it?

(Outside, the sound of an ambulance approaching and pulling up.)

JESS. *(Surveying the flight case.)* Including that bloody great 3D printer?

ALISON. Yes. That's in there.

JESS. The one I could scarcely lift?

(The 1992 doorbell rings.)

ALISON. I dismantled it first. I've told you, you should work out more often.

JESS. I don't need to work out, I'm a researcher. Researchers don't need to, it's in their contract.

ALISON. Nor do CGI Graphic Designers but it helps.

JESS. Only in their imaginations.

(The sound of a paramedic's voice from the hall. The usual squawk of RT chatter in the background.)

VOICE. *(Talking to a child.)* Hello, darling, we've come to see to your Mum, okay? Can you show us where she is? What, upstairs, is she? Would you like to lead on, then? It's all right, you're not to worry, we'll take care of her from here, darling, not to worry...

JESS. So you won't be needing your old desk in there, either.

ALISON. Not now I've got the new one, no.

JESS. *(Indicating the writing desk.)* Tell you what, you could always have this one.

ALISON. *(Smiles.)* My mother said she remembered my grandmother sitting here at the end of every week, desperately trying to balance the housekeeping. Grandfather standing over her, tapping his foot.

(She perches on a flight case.)

(During the next, the two removal men (very different in appearance from the previous pair!) enter and gradually start removing all the furniture until only the flight cases remain. They enter at this point and take out the sideboard, during the next, through the hall doorway.)

She was a very tragic case really. A victim of her time, in a way.

JESS. Your grandmother?

ALISON. Well, her as well. No, I was talking about my mother. I mean I remember her now as this terrible drunk who kept dropping things and continually falling over but she was apparently a really bright kid, according to my uncle Richard. Uncle Dickie. Whom I've totally lost touch with these days, apart from an occasional Christmas card. But after Mother died he did write me this sweet note. When they were together at their first school, she was the star pupil from all accounts. At one stage there were great plans for her but, in the end, it all came to nothing. Despite the headmistress's and her mother's best efforts.

(The removal men have returned from the hall and now take up the sofa which, during the next they take out, again through the hall.)

JESS. *(Sitting beside her on the other case.)* What happened?

ALISON. Wrong sex, darling, wrong sex, wasn't she? Uncle Dickie said she gradually realised she was fighting a losing battle. Ten years old she was gifted and brilliant, by the time she was fifteen she'd grown average, ordinary and smoking dope. Bypassed university, managed to scrape her way into teachers' training college. Shortly afterwards, she got pregnant and that was that. I think to be fair to him, Uncle Dickie must have felt a teeny bit guilty having appropriated the lion's share of the family budget for his own education. I mean he's done pretty well for himself and he's got a nice job at Boots the chemists and a nice family but, let's be honest, he's never going to discover the cure for cancer.

(The removal men return and remove the armchair and coffee table during the next.)

Mind you, one way or another, she certainly got her own back on the world, my sweet stoned, hippy mother. *(She reflects.)* Oh, God, it's all coming back now, it's all coming back to me! Did I ever tell you about my tenth birthday party?

JESS. I don't think so, no.

ALISON. *(Smiling.)* Hardly her finest hour, I'm afraid. She went to so much trouble, too. It was shortly before Dad finally walked out on us. She was determined to give me the best, the most wonderful birthday party ever, whether he turned out or not, sod him. I think she knew it meant a lot to me that he was actually there so she pretended he was coming. Though I suspect he never had any intention of turning up.

(The removal men return and remove the desk and chair. The room is now devoid of furniture.)

(During this.) She spent days beforehand shut away in the kitchen, just like a normal mother, whisking and baking and mixing. She was quite the world's worst cook. She even went so far as to pay Jennifer Bainbridge from the village to come in and help supervise, poor kid. Mummy really pulled out all the stops, bless her. Considering she really felt as much at home in the kitchen as I do.

JESS. That's saying something.

ALISON. Steady, now! Remember my omelette. You're forgetting my omelette.

JESS. Oh, yes. I do beg its pardon. Omelette singular. Definitely a one-off. Never to be repeated. Well, that's not quite true, it repeated on me most of the night actually...

ALISON. I'm ignoring all this. Do you want to hear about my birthday party, or not?

JESS. Sorry, yes, carry on. Your mother was slaving away in the kitchen...

ALISON. Jellies, little cakes, sausage rolls, you name it... But her pride and joy, the real centrepiece was this giant trifle, made with her own fair hands. Her own speciality. Topped with God knows how much whipped cream. Sponge cake, custard, fruit, the lot. All sprinkled with a liberal dosage of LSD.

JESS. What? For a kids' party? You must have all been high as kites!

ALISON. We were, most of us. The ones that weren't sick as dogs…

JESS. Including you, presumably?

(The removal men return and take away one of the flight cases which leaves **JESS** *standing.)*

ALISON. No, I was fine. I'd developed a sort of immunity to drugs by then, thanks to my hippy mother. I probably actually emerged from her womb in a cloud of cannabis smoke. Which explains why I've never touched the stuff. *(To the the two removal men.)* – Do be careful, loading that, won't you –? But as you can imagine the scene in the dining room was like the aftermath of a Roman orgy. Consequently there was a certain frosty indignation when the parents finally came to collect their kids. Especially from a certain Councillor Penfold who took serious offence at the state of his beloved stoned offspring – Justin Penfold, nasty little bully, I recall – my mother and his father nearly came to blows and it ended up with her rushing outside and smashing the headlights of his smart new Mercedes. They settled out of court eventually. My father paid the damages.

JESS. Happy birthday to you, then. No, you never told me that. I can't imagine why you didn't. Must have been buried very deep.

ALISON. I was suddenly reminded of it, seeing that van out there.

JESS. The removal van?

ALISON. What's written on the side there. That's exactly what my mother shouted at Councillor Penfold as he drove away on his sidelights.

*(**JESS** laughs.)*

(The removal men return for the final case.)

I had to face them all the next day, of course, my friends – my ex-friends rather – and classmates. Most of whom were forbidden to speak to me. Some of them even asked me to give them their presents back.

JESS. I hope you didn't.

ALISON. Only the ones I didn't want.

(The removal men wait.)

(She rises and releases the case.)

(To the removal men.) That's okay. You can take this one now. Do be careful with it, it's very delicate, some of it.

(The removal men finally leave.)

(Vainly calling after them.) I say... excuse me...

JESS. What's the problem?

ALISON. Do remind them I'm travelling with them, won't you? I don't want them leaving without me...

*(**JESS** hurries after them.)*

JESS. *(As she goes, calling.)* Hang on! Hang on a tick! Hello?

*(**ALISON** is left alone in the empty room. She stands in the centre of it, as if replaying old memories.)*

ALISON. *(Eventually, softly to herself.)* Goodbye, room. Goodbye, house.

(A moment.)

(From outside, the furniture van horn blows, bringing her out of her reverie.)

(She turns and leaves the room through the hall. As she does so, the lights fade to a...)

(Blackout.)

End of Play

Milton Keynes UK
Ingram Content Group UK Ltd.
UKHW020617120923
428513UK00014B/438

9 780573 000256